HISTORY OF BRITAIN

THE SAXONS & VIKINGS

406 to 1066

Revised and updated

Brenda Williams

Heinemann
LIBRARY

www.heinemann.co.uk/library
Visit our website to find out more information about Heinemann Library books.

To order:
☎ Phone 44 (0) 1865 888112
🖹 Send a fax to 44 (0) 1865 314091
🖥 Visit the Heinemann bookshop at www.heinemann.co.uk/library to browse our catalogue and order online.

First published in Great Britain by Heinemann Library, Halley Court, Jordan Hill, Oxford OX2 8EJ, part of Harcourt Education.
Heinemann is a registered trademark of Harcourt Education Ltd.

© Harcourt Education Ltd 1994, 2006
First published in paperback in 2007
The moral right of the proprietor has been asserted.

Editorial: Lionel Bender and Richard Woodham
Design: Ben White and Michelle Lisseter
Picture Research: Jennie Karrach and Mica Brancic
Production: Helen McCreath

Originated by RMW
Printed and bound in Hong Kong, China, by Wing King Tong.

ISBN 978 0 431 10810 0 (hardback)
10 09 08 07 06
10 9 8 7 6 5 4 3 2 1

ISBN 978 0 431 10819 3 (paperback)
11 10 09 08 07
10 9 8 7 6 5 4 3 2 1

British Library Cataloguing in Publication Data
Williams, Brenda
Saxons & Vikings – 2nd ed. – (History of Britain)
941'.01
A full catalogue record for this book is available from the British Library.

Acknowledgements
The publishers would like to thank the following for permission to reproduce photographs:
Page 7: Mick Sharp/E. Yorks Archaeological Trust; Page 9: Mick Sharp/Jean Williamson; Page 10: C. M. Dixon; Page 12: Mick Sharp/E. Yorks Archaeological Trust; Page 14 (top, bottom): Trustees of the British Museum; Page 16: A. F. Kersting; Page 17: Trinity College Library, Dublin/ Mss 57, fol. 21v; Page 18 (top): Ashmolean Museum, Oxford; Page 18 (bottom): Aerofilms Ltd; Page 21: York Archaeological Trust; Page 22: Mick Sharp; Page 24: Werner Forman Archive/Statens Historiska Museum, Stockholm; Page 25: British Library/Mss No. Cott Vesp. A.I. folio 30v; Page 27: c The Pierpont Morgan Library, New York 1994/M.736, f.12; Page 28: Ashmolean Museum, Oxford; Page 29: British Library/Mss No. Cott IB BV, folio 6v; Page 31: British Library/Mss No. Cott IB BV folio 5 detail; Page 32: Ashmolean Museum, Oxford; Page 34: York Archaeological Trust; Page 36: British Library/Mss No. Claud BIV, folio 59; Page 37 (top): Michael Holford; Page 37 (bottom): Mick Sharp; Page 39 (left): Ashmolean Museum, Oxford; Page 39 (right): British Library/Mss No. Stowe 944, folio 6; Page 40: British Library/Mss No. Cott. Vit c111, folio 56v; Page 41, 42–43, 43 (top): Michael Holford.

Illustrations by: James Field: 8/9, 20/21, 22/23, 30/31, 32/33, 34/35, 38/39, 43, 46; John James: 6/7, 10/11, 12/13, 18/19, 26/27, 28/29, 36/37; Mark Bergin: 14/15, 24/25; Bill Donohoe: 16/17.

Cover photograph of the King Alfred the Great statue in Hampshire, reproduced with permission of Alamy/ Peter Titmuss.

The publishers would like to thank Andrew Langley for his assistance in the preparation of this book.

Every effort has been made to contact copyright holders of any material reproduced in this book. Any omissions will be rectified in subsequent printings if notice is given to the publishers.

CONTENTS

Unfamiliar words are explained in the **glossary** *on page 46*

ABOUT THIS BOOK

This book considers Saxon and Viking Britain chronologically, meaning that events are described in the order in which they happened, from AD 406 to 1066. However, most of the double-page articles deal with a particular aspect of everyday life, such as farming, trade, houses, and food. These things did not change very much over the centuries.

On page 45 there are lists of the rulers of Britain from about 800 and a map of Saxon kingdoms. There is also an explanation of how many modern place names come from Saxon and Viking words. The book uses the terms "Britons" and "British" to refer to the original inhabitants rather than the newcomers.

Unfamiliar words are explained in the glossary on page 46.

▼ **This map** shows the location of places mentioned in the text. The places on the map include large towns, small towns, sites of famous battles, famous ruins, and places of interest.

ROMAN BRITAIN
55 BC to AD 406

SAXONS AND VIKINGS
406 to 1066

MEDIEVAL BRITAIN
1066 to 1485

THE TUDORS
1485 to 1603

THE STUARTS
1603 to 1714

GEORGIAN BRITAIN
1714 to 1837

VICTORIAN BRITAIN
1837 to 1901

MODERN BRITAIN
1901 to today

INTRODUCTION

From the 5th to the 11th centuries, Britain was repeatedly invaded by peoples from Europe. It was a long period of change. The Roman army, needed to fight hostile tribes elsewhere, had left Britain by AD 410. Soon after, peoples from northwest Europe crossed the sea to settle there. Among them were Angles, Saxons, and Jutes. The newcomers drove the Britons of the south and east northward and westward to Strathclyde, Cornwall, and Wales. Angles and Saxons settled in south, east, and central Britain and became the "English". Further north lived the Picts, and the Scots, who came from Ireland. Britain was split into many small kingdoms that fought each other for power. In time, rulers of the large English kingdoms became the strongest. In the 800s, more invaders came to Britain. Vikings from Norway and Denmark came at first to burn and loot, but then settled to a peaceful way of life. In 1066, the last Saxon king of England was killed by new invaders, the Normans from France.

All the invaders of Britain brought their own languages, laws, customs, and religions. We know something of their lives from coins, jewellery, household objects, and remains of buildings of the time that archaeologists find in the ground. No Saxon or Viking invader left any writings, but some of their history was later written down by Christian monks. The most useful to us of such books are Bede's *Ecclesiastical History of the English People* of 731, and the *Anglo-Saxon Chronicle* from the 800s to 1154.

Much of the story told in the following pages is about England, because that is where the Saxons and Vikings mainly settled. Similarly, "Saxons" or "Anglo-Saxons" is used for Angles, Saxons, Jutes, and other settlers of the period. Some of these peoples' customs, laws, and language are still part of English life. Names they called places in their new land are still in use today.

BRITAIN AFTER THE ROMANS

"Hengist and Horsa, invited by Vortigern, king of the Britons, landed... at first in aid of the Britons, but afterwards they fought against them". Stories like this explained how the Saxons came to live in Britain. A monk called Bede wrote them down around 731. He said the Saxons arrived in 449.

The first of the "English" came from north Germany and Denmark. They were a mix of peoples including Angles, Saxons, Jutes, Frisians, and Franks. These seafarers and warriors came to trade and raid in Britain before 400. The island's Roman rulers built forts along the coasts to keep the pirates away. Some Saxons joined the Roman army to fight off other Saxon raiders.

Around 408, the Romans and their army left Britain. Many Britons noticed little change at first. Others were soon to lose their lands or their lives.

The invaders crossed the North Sea in long, narrow ships. Roman shore forts such as Reculver and Porchester on the south coast now stood empty. The invaders rowed up rivers and creeks, and into the heart of Britain.
- Each ship carried about 40 men.
- The man at the back of the ship steered with a long oar.
- Saxons used short swords called seaxes, from which the name "Saxons" came.

▽ **The Anglo-Saxon invaders came to Britain** from the lowlands of north Germany and Denmark.
● The Angles settled in East Anglia, the Midlands, and Northumbria.
● The Saxons settled the south of England. They formed the kingdoms of: Sussex (the South Saxons), Wessex (West Saxons), Essex (East Saxons), and Middlesex (Middle Saxons).
● Jutes from Jutland (Denmark) settled in Kent, Hampshire and the Isle of Wight.
● Frisians and Franks joined the invasions.

△ **The skull and upper skeleton of a Saxon** found in a grave at Thwing in Yorkshire, Beside the head lay beads of amber and blue glass. The little we know of the early Saxons in England comes mainly from grave finds like this. People were buried with some of their possessions, such as jewellery and items of clothing.

Picts and Scots attacked from the north. And across the North Sea came invading Saxon ships. British leaders, like Vortigern, hired other Saxons such as Hengist and Horsa to help fight off the invaders. The Britons paid these men in money and land. Some demanded more, or took what they wanted.

More and more invaders arrived, but now they came to find land to farm. They sailed their long narrow boats up rivers to reach deep inland. They forced the Britons from the land they wanted, or made them slaves.

At first they drove the Britons further and further west. Then around 500, the Britons seem to have won several victories. One of their leaders was Ambrosius Aurelianus, and one of their victories was at a place called Mons Badonicus, or Mount Badon. This may have been at Badbury Rings in Dorset. The main leader of the Britons at this time may have been the warrior later called King Arthur. For a while at least, the Saxons were halted.

THE SAXONS SETTLE

The Saxon leaders found good land to farm in the river valleys, and shared it out among their followers. The new farmers cut down trees, ploughed the soil, and built themselves sturdy wooden houses. Settlements grew up.

△ **Anglo-Saxons**. Some leaders became kings. Their noble warriors were called thanes. Thanes were usually given land by the king, and freemen farmers (above left) called churls rented land from them. Some farm workers were slaves. Christian missionaries (above centre) came after the invaders had settled.

◁ △ **A 5th-century Saxon settlement**. It had buildings of wood and thatch and usually a wooden outer fence. Farm animals included:
● horses to ride and pull carts
● oxen, up to eight in a team, to pull the plough
● dogs to drive sheep and guard against wolves.
    At first, those who worked on the farms made all they needed. Settlements later had craftsmen.

Some farmers settled on lands seized from the Britons. Others cleared forests to grow crops and make pasture for cattle and sheep. Goats, pigs, and horses grazed on heathlands. Pigs also rooted in woods for acorns and beech nuts.

The Saxons sowed crops of wheat, rye, oats, and barley. They also grew peas, beans, and lentils. Farmers divided large open fields into long strips, which they shared. They also shared a big wheeled plough and the oxen to pull it. It was hard work turning round the heavy plough at the end of the field. Long strips of land meant making fewer turns.

The first settlements were groups of three or four family farms. Houses, farm buildings, and workshops were all made of wood and had sloping thatched roofs. Around the settlement was a fence to protect it from wolves or enemies.

In time the settlements became villages. Most had a meeting place for the villagers. It might be an open space, or the large hall of a local leader. The first Saxon chiefs were the men who had led the settlers to Britain and given them land. In return the farmers worked and fought for their lord. The bonds between family members and between a man and his lord were especially important in Anglo-Saxon life.

◁ **Cremation urn** found at Spong Hill in Norfolk, which was the site of an Anglo-Saxon settlement similar to that shown opposite. Thousands of English villages and towns began as Saxon settlements.

SAXONS AT HOME

Bede describes Saxons feasting together at home: "They sat long at supper and drank hard, with a great fire in the middle of the room. It happened that the sparks flew up and caught the top of the house, which being made of wattle (woven twigs) and thatch, was presently in flame".

Most Saxon homes rotted away long ago. But traces of the wooden posts that held them up can still be seen in the soil. Using these signs, archaeologists have worked out what the buildings looked like and have rebuilt a whole settlement at West Stow in Suffolk. We know what Saxons wore and used in their homes from remains found in their graves.

The poorest homes were much like those built by Britons before Roman times. Families often shared them with their animals, with just a low wall or thin wooden screen between. There were no chimneys or windows. A fire burned in the middle of the floor. Houses were lit by candles or pottery lamps burning animal fat. Some had earth floors. Others had dug-out floors, covered by wooden boards.

▽ **Saxon craftsmen** made beautifully decorated metalwork and jewellery of glass, amber, crystal, and garnets. People wore brooches for fastening clothes. Saxon brooches were saucer-shaped, like the one below. Angles had long brooches. Women wore strings of beads across their chests or round their waists.

▷ **Inside a Saxon house.** There was little furniture, Some people had a table, and benches used for both sitting and sleeping on. Families often ate and slept on the floor. Wood from about 18 oak trees was needed to build a Saxon house.

Items used in cooking and preparing foods included:
● a large cooking pot hung on a chain from roof beams over the fire.
● water-bottles, bowls, and large storage jars.
● buckets, to carry water for drinking and cooking from a stream or lake.

△▷ **In early Saxon settlements, people generally made their own household items**. Saxons made pots by hand, as above, until they began using a potter's wheel in the 7th century. Carpenters made wooden items using chisels and a lathe (a turning machine).

At West Stow, iron knives, bone combs, and drinking cups and pots, like those shown right, have all been found.

Women spun sheep's wool and wove it into cloth. They used plant dyes to colour it, and made long tunic dresses for themselves. Men wore short tunics and thick wool trousers. They tied on their leather shoes with straps that criss-crossed up the leg.

Women ground grain, baked bread and brewed beer from barley. They cooked over the fire. Saxons enjoyed meat, especially pork, and fish. But their daily food was bread, cheese, milk, and eggs. Children helped at home and on the farm. They gathered firewood, watched over the grazing animals, scared birds from newly sown fields, fed hens, and collected eggs.

KINGS AND KINGDOMS

By 600, Saxon settlements had become small kingdoms. The most important were: East Anglia, Essex, Kent, Sussex, Mercia, Northumbria, and Wessex. At times one king grew powerful enough to be bretwalda, or overlord, of the whole country.

The first Saxon "kings" were the chiefs who led the invaders. Bede says they were Hengist and Horsa in Kent, Aelle in Sussex, and Cerdic and Cynric in Wessex. By 560, Kent had become the first important English kingdom. It was ruled until 616 by Ethelbert, whose capital (main settlement) was at Canterbury. His people traded with the Franks of Europe, and his laws are the oldest we know of among the Saxons. Later, Northumbria became the most powerful kingdom. Its king was Edwin. A Saxon palace, or hall, found at Yeavering in Northumberland was probably his. Each king moved through his kingdom from one hall to another. While he stayed there with his followers, they feasted with him and swore to be loyal to him in battle. In return he gave them gifts of land and riches.

▷ **Cut-away of a great hall of a Saxon king.** Such a hall is described in the poem Beowulf, written in about 750: "The hall towered up, lofty and wide-gabled... Woven hangings gleamed, gold-adorned, on the walls".

"King" – "cyning" in Old English – means man of family. Any man of the royal family could be king if he gained enough supporters. This led to feuds and war.
● In time of war, a king called up all men to fight for him. Early Saxon farmers kept their weapons ready at home.
● In Saxon law a person's life was worth a set amount of money. This wergild, or "man-money", had to be paid to a victim's family by his killer. A king's life might be worth six times that of a thane.

▽ **Unearthing remains of a Saxon hall** at Thwing, Yorkshire. Dark patches in the soil show where the wooden posts stood.

▽ **The king's followers** included older, trusted men who generally stayed at home. Young men stayed with the king as his bodyguard.

They hoped for rich rewards when feasting and drinking with him in the hall.

By day, the king and his companions went out to hunt, ride or race horses, or settle local disputes. At Yeavering there was a wooden seating area like a grandstand that could hold 320 people. King Edwin may have held meetings here with his advisors.

◁ **A Saxon hall belonged to a thane or king.** At Yeavering there were several halls. The largest was 24 metres long and 12 metres wide. Halls like these have been reconstructed in Denmark.

THE SUTTON HOO SHIP

Saxon poets called kings "treasure-givers". When a king died, he was buried with some of his riches and a mound of earth was piled on top to mark his grave. In 1939, archaeologists opened a Saxon mound at Sutton Hoo in Suffolk and found a treasure ship.

The ship's timbers had rotted away in the earth but its shape was clear. It was an open boat nearly 30 metres long. In the centre was a hoard of gold, silver, and decorated jewellery that could only have belonged to a lord or king.

Everyday items like cups, combs, knives and buckets lay with the war-gear of a splendid warrior. There were mystery objects that may have been the symbols of kingship, but no traces of a body.

The Sutton Hoo ship-burial was one of the richest finds made by archaeologists in Britain. It proved the wealth of an East Anglian ruler – but which one?

▷ **Men pulled the ship up** from the River Deben to the burial ground at Sutton Hoo. They laid it in a trench, put grave goods on board, filled in the soil, then made an earth mound.

▷ **Photograph taken in 1939 of the excavation at Sutton Hoo** near Woodbridge in Suffolk. Many of the 20 mounds at Sutton Hoo had been robbed long ago. Robbers had also dug into Redwald's mound and lit a fire, but then left.

The archaeologists dug out the objects and photographed the site. They sent the finds away to be studied, and filled in the trench. Sutton Hoo's owner gave the treasures to the British Museum.

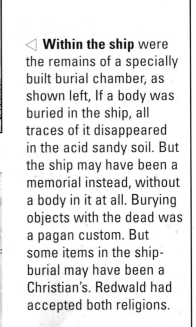

◁ **Within the ship** were the remains of a specially built burial chamber, as shown left, If a body was buried in the ship, all traces of it disappeared in the acid sandy soil. But the ship may have been a memorial instead, without a body in it at all. Burying objects with the dead was a pagan custom. But some items in the ship-burial may have been a Christian's. Redwald had accepted both religions.

◁ **Buried at Sutton Hoo were:**
- a lyre – a stringed musical instrument – and ivory gaming pieces
- an iron helmet, with bird-shaped nose, moustache and eyebrows (shown left)
- a sword, shield, spear, mail shirt, and axe-hammer
- a gold belt buckle, jewelled purse, shoulder clasps for leather armour, gold and garnet jewellery
- a stone sceptre and royal standard.

Gold coins in the mound seem to show that the owner was Redwald, who died around 627. Bede says that Redwald was bretwalda between Ethelbert of Kent and Edwin of Northumbria. The coins were from Gaul (France), but some objects had come from Byzantium (now Istanbul) and Egypt. Some finds tell us more about the East Anglian kings. The great helmet and shield were decorated in a Swedish style. Since ship-burials have also been found in Sweden, it seems that the East Anglian royal family – the Wuffingas – may have come from Sweden in the 6th century. By the 7th century they held power for a while over all the English.

SAXONS AND SAINTS

In Roman times, most Britons were Christians. When they fled from the Saxons, they set up small churches in Wales and the west. Monks from these and other Celtic churches later took Christianity to the Saxons, who were pagans. Missionaries sent by the Pope in Rome came to convert the Saxons of southern England.

◁ **Celtic monks** on the Irish island of Skellig Michael lived in beehive-shaped stone huts, or cells. They owned little, and spent their lives in thought and prayer.

▷ **The Northumbrian Ruthwell Cross**, now preserved in a church in Scotland. It is carved with scenes, runes, and a Saxon poem about the life of Jesus Christ.

▷ **The monastery at Jarrow**, Northumbria, was where Bede the historian lived. Monks worked in the monastery gardens, fields, and workshops. During the day, they prayed every 2 or 3 hours. During the night, they rose at least once to say prayers.

Monasteries were the only Saxon schools. Bede entered a monastery in about 680, when he was 7 years old. Two years later he moved to Jarrow. He became a priest, teacher, scholar, and author of many books. He sent people all over Britain to collect information about the history of the Angles and Saxons.

◁▷ **Books had to be copied and illustrated by hand.** The painting, left, is from the *Book of Durrow*, made in the 7th century in Ireland, Monks wrote on parchment, a material made from animal skins, and decorated the pages in bright colours.

Patrick, a British monk, introduced Christianity to Ireland before 460. Facts about his life are few. One story tells how he was seized by pirates and taken to Ireland as a slave. He escaped and later went back there to teach and set up monasteries. Irish monks often lived in lonely places, in small buildings of stone.

Around 563 a monk named Columba left Ireland for the isle of Iona near Scotland and started a monastery there. Monks from Iona then converted most of Scotland. Another monk, Aidan, went to found the monastery of Lindisfarne off Northumbria in 635. These holy men and the people who followed them are known as Celtic Christians.

The missionaries from Rome had arrived in Kent in 597. King Ethelred met their leader Augustine in the open air, where he hoped the priest's "magic" would do less harm. The mission was successful and St Augustine became first Archbishop of Canterbury. Over the next 90 years, all the Saxon kingdoms gradually accepted the new religion.

Leaders of Roman and Celtic Christians met at Whitby in 663 to settle disagreements over religious matters. This brought the English Church closer to the Church on the Continent.

BORDER BATTLES

Northumbria and Mercia struggled for power as their leaders feuded and fought to gain kingdoms. The most ruthless won. "You know how much blood his father shed to secure the kingdom on his son", said the scholar Alcuin about Offa, king of Mercia.

The Northumbrian kings – Edwin, Oswald, and Oswy – were overlords of the English from about 616 to 657. But to stay strong they needed more lands and wealth to give to their followers. On their southern border lay Mercia. To the west in Wales were the British kingdoms of Gwynedd, Dyfed, Powys, and Gwent. King Penda of Mercia and Cadwallon of Gwynedd joined forces in 632 to fight the Northumbrians – and they won.

Northumbrian and Mercian kings slew each other by turns, until Mercia won a vital battle near the River Trent in 679. Mercian kings had already overcome the neighbouring Midland tribes and now became overlords of most of the English south of the River Humber.

△ **Offa ordered millions of silver pennies to be made** like the one above. They were bigger and thinner than earlier coins. Most bore his name and face, but a few had those of his queen, Cynethryth.

▷ **Offa's Dyke**
● stretched for about 180 kilometres along Mercia's western border with Wales
● stood over 7 metres high, in front of a ditch that was 2 metres deep
● was constructed mainly of wooden poles and piled-up earth
● was built to stop Welsh raids into Mercia after Offa's attacks on Wales.
    The photo, right, shows part of Offa's Dyke today.

When Offa began his reign over Mercia in 757, he was already the most powerful Saxon king ever. About 780, he overcame the south-east kingdoms of Kent, Surrey, Sussex, and Wessex. By so doing, he controlled the growing trade in England and with the Continent.

Later, Offa was acknowledged as the first king of the English. He was respected abroad, too. He was the only ruler in western Europe to be treated as an equal by Charlemagne, king of the Franks. Offa's silver "pennies" formed the pattern for English money long after.

Offa's power is shown by the great border barrier he built between Mercia and Wales – Offa's Dyke. But Mercia weakened after his death in 796, and little remains from his reign. Most of Offa's written laws and charters were lost in the turmoil that the English faced after 787, when the Vikings arrived.

▽ **Offa's England**. The map below shows Offa's Dyke and the lands he had influence over. On the borders of the Saxon kingdoms lay smaller British-held lands, such as Dumnonia, which the Saxons gradually took over. In the north, the Picts and the Scots from Ireland were rivals, struggling for territory.

◁ **Saxon soldiers** watch as the wooden fence is put in place on top of Offa's Dyke. In the background, other soldiers march away a group of slaves who have been working on the dyke. It probably took more than 5,000 men in all to build the barrier.

THE COMING OF THE VIKINGS

"In this year (787)... first came three ships of Northmen, out of Denmark... These were the first ships of Danishmen which sought the land of the English nation." So the *Anglo-Saxon Chronicle* described the coming of the Vikings to Britain. Some came to find land to settle. Others came to steal, burn, and slay.

▷ **The Vikings raided the coasts of Europe** in their longships. Each ship could carry 60 men. Later armies of Vikings came in fleets of up to 350 ships. A longship:
● was about 25 metres long
● was made mainly of oak wood with deck, oars, and mast of pine
● had a square sail
● was powered in calm weather or on rivers by rowers with long oars
● with sail set and in a good wind, could travel 200 kilometres in a day.

Who were these Northmen or Vikings? They came from Scandinavia, the lands we call Norway, Sweden, and Denmark.

They were farmers, fishermen, seafarers, traders – and fierce fighters. Their lands in forests and mountains were too hard to farm for an easy living. They were expert boat-builders, sailing the coastal fjords of their homeland in sturdy wooden ships. Some Vikings went far west across the ocean, guided by the Sun and stars and by the flight of birds. Viking adventurers hoped to grow rich – by trade or by plunder.

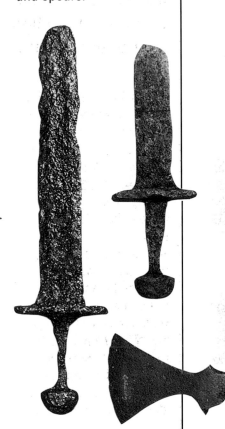

▽ **Two Viking swords with double blades, and an axe head.** Viking warriors also used a long knife known as a scramasaxe, bows, and spears.

△ **In Scandinavia, some Vikings lived in trading towns.** Excavations at Hedeby (Denmark) and Birka (Sweden) show us that:
● houses were wooden, with straw or turf roofs
● ships came by fiord or river to unload
● traders set up stalls to buy and sell goods
● craftworkers made leather goods, jewellery, pottery, and tools
● around the town were an earth wall and a fence.

Why did the Vikings roam? There was not enough land at home for every young man to have a share. Younger sons would not inherit the family farm, but by travelling and raiding they could become rich in gold and slaves.

There was much to steal in Britain: the treasures of kings and monasteries, and plenty of silver coins. Its rulers were neither strong nor united. Northumbria was the kingdom most famous for monastic wealth, and in the 700s it was becoming weaker. The other kingdoms and kings fought among themselves.

In 787 three Viking ships from Denmark landed in Dorset. The local reeve (a royal official) greeted the newcomers. Thinking they were traders, he told them they must speak to the king. Instead, they killed the reeve, then sailed away.

For 793, the *Anglo-Saxon Chronicle* records that terrified Northumbrians saw omens: whirlwinds, lightning and dragons in the skies. The "storm" broke when Northmen raided the monastery at Lindisfarne in Northumbria. They burned its buildings, stole its treasures, and slaughtered the defenceless monks.

BOLD SEAFARERS

The Viking raid on Lindisfarne was the first of many. For the next hundred years there were wars in England between English and Northmen. But in the north and west of the British Isles, the Northmen settled more peacefully. They founded small farming communities like those in Scandinavia.

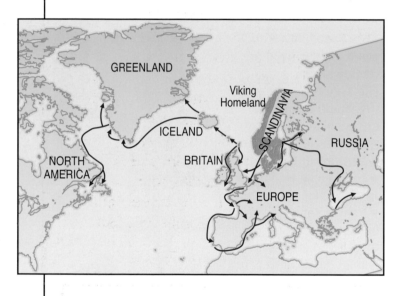

◁△ **Viking voyages and settlements**, like the one above, between AD 800 and 1000.

The Vikings were not just pirates. They were also traders and settlers who journeyed far across the sea and overland. A Viking band might trade furs for slaves on one voyage, and loot a church's gold on another. Next time they might seek good pasture for sheep.

The first Vikings to land in Britain were Danes. Most of those who followed were Norwegians. Vikings from Norway sailed to Scotland and settled the Orkney and Shetland islands in the 800s.

The first Viking raid on Ireland was in 795. Ireland became a centre of Viking trade, particularly in slaves, and piracy. Irish Viking settlements included Waterford, Wexford and Dublin, which became an important trading town.

▷ **Viking settlers in northern Britain** lived much as they had in their homelands. They:
● ploughed small fields to grow wheat, oats, rye, and barley
● stored hay to feed sheep and cattle in winter
● built wooden boats and boat sheds
● caught fish which was smoked, salted, or dried
● made long, low houses usually of stone and with roofs of straw thatch or turf laid over wooden beams. The photo above shows the remains of several Viking houses at Jarlshof on the Shetland Islands.

Vikings drove the Picts and Scots from some northern islands, the Isle of Man, and parts of mainland Scotland. They settled to a life of farming and fishing. They planted cereals and vegetables, and kept cows, sheep, goats, pigs, and chickens. Viking families brought their farm animals overseas in sturdy boats called knorrs. Some of the men married local women.

A whole family (grandparents, parents, children, even aunts and uncles) often shared a one-room house. They cooked their food in an iron cauldron hung above a fire. They drank beer (made from barley) and mead, from cups made of horn. They wore woollen clothes, coloured with dyes made from plants. They made shoes, boots, and belts from leather. Blacksmiths made iron tools and weapons. Carvers made combs and fish hooks from bone.

△ **The Picts and Scots** sometimes used ancient Celtic hill-forts, like this one at Rockliffe in Dumfries, to defend themselves against the Vikings. In 870, Vikings from Ireland came to Scotland in a fleet of longships and laid siege for 4 months to a large Pictish fortress on Dunbarton Rock in Strathclyde. The Picts surrendered, and most were taken to Ireland to be sold as slaves.

△ **A Viking warrior's** sword, axe, and spear. A good sword was a family treasure, passed from father to son. Axe heads were decorated with intricate patterns.

GODS OF THE NORTH

In their homelands, Saxons and Vikings both worshipped the Norse gods. These were the gods of warriors, whose heroic deeds were told at feasts in the king's hall. In England, Saxons and Vikings later became Christians, but did not forget their old religious beliefs and stories.

△ **A Viking tapestry shows Odin, Thor, and Frigg.** Odin the one-eyed was chief of the Norse gods. Frigg was his wife.

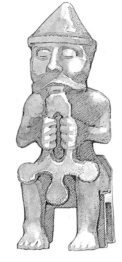

△ **A bronze statue of Thor** with his hammer. Lightning flashed as he flung his hammer against enemies.

▷ **Sword-making in the smithy.** A blacksmith hammers red-hot metal rods together to make a blade. Some swords had runes or charms written on them, to give them magic powers. Smiths kept their skills secret.

On the blacksmith's workbench is a mould with the shapes of Thor's hammer and a Christian cross. This shows how the Saxons and Vikings often kept their pagan customs alongside their new Christian ones.

Saxons and Vikings shared many gods, using slightly different names for each one. Saxon Woden was the Viking Odin, chief among the gods. The Saxon gods Tiw, Woden, Thunor (Thor), and Frigg give us the names of Tuesday, Wednesday, Thursday, and Friday. A Saxon spring goddess – Eostre – gave her name to the Christian festival of Easter.

Saxons used spells and charms against evil spirits and sickness. They wrote them down in "magic" runes, or letters. They believed that rocks, trees, and springs had spirits. They feared witches, demons, and goblins – and dark, gloomy places where horrible monsters might lurk. An English Christian called Guthlac described the creatures he said he saw in his room on a lonely marsh. These "wicked sprites" had "filthy beards, shaggy ears... horses' teeth... scabby thighs, knotty knees, crooked legs,... splay feet."

Vikings believed that Fate ruled their lives. Three goddesses called Norns looked after the past, the present, and the future. Norns also fixed the fate of every child at birth. The goddess Frigg made crops grow, Freyja, goddess of love, had a chariot drawn by cats.

△ **Picture from a Saxon manuscript of a king with his musicians.** Saxons enjoyed listening to long poems recited by bards, or minstrels, The poems, like *Beowulf* and *The Battle of Maldon*, were often about the deeds of warriors and gods.

The Viking gods lived in a place called Asgard, which was joined to Earth by a rainbow bridge. Around the Earth was an ocean full of monsters, and beyond the ocean lived the Frost Giants. These were the enemies of the gods, who would one day destroy them in battle.

Death in battle meant everlasting glory to a Viking. Chosen warriors went to Odin's heavenly hall of Valhalla, to fight by day and feast by night.

Many Vikings believed that a person's spirit sailed to the next world in a ship, and some Vikings were buried in a ship under an earth mound. Others were placed on a boat that was set alight. Both Saxons and Vikings believed in an after-life. Their families placed in their graves all the things they would need with them, such as weapons and coins.

THE DANES MOVE INTO ENGLAND

In the mid 800s, large armies of Vikings (called Danes by the English) attacked western Europe, and England in particular. The *Anglo-Saxon Chronicle* says: "There was warfare and sorrow over England." Wessex was the only English kingdom with the will and the leaders to fight off the invaders.

▽ **Vikings plundered London and Canterbury in 851.**
● London's Roman walls were no defence against the Vikings, although the English lined the river bank with stakes to try to keep the ships from landing (as shown below).
● By 871, the Vikings controlled the Thames valley from Reading to the sea, with all London's trade.

In the 830s, Vikings raided the Isle of Sheppey in Kent, the south coast and East Anglia. In 851, a fleet of 350 Viking ships appeared at the mouth of the River Thames. The English had no navy to fight them. The men guarding London's old Roman walls could do little to stop the invaders, who plundered the town. Canterbury was also attacked. Also in 851, Vikings camped in Thanet for the winter, the first time they had stayed in England after the fighting season.

◁ **Viking raiders** had always sailed away with their stolen goods. But the "Great Army" that landed in 865 stayed in England,

The army had many kings and jarls (lords), but there was no single Viking general. Bands of warriors followed their own leaders, who were often their ships' captains.

△ **Edmund, king of East Anglia**, was killed by Vikings in 869. This manuscript illustration, dating from about 1130, shows the Vikings dragging the king from his throne. Edmund's death, probably by ritual torture, made him a Christian martyr. He was buried at the place later named Bury St Edmunds.

The biggest Viking army yet seen in England landed in 865. It conquered East Anglia, Northumbria, and Mercia. Monasteries were burned and their monks killed or driven away. The English Church was in danger of collapse.

Hoards of coins buried at this time show how panic spread as the Viking army swept through eastern and northern England. This was more than a raid. The invaders had come to stay.

In the south, Ethelred I, king of Wessex, and his brother, Alfred, fought fierce battles against the Vikings. Churchmen fought, too. In 871 Ethelred died and Alfred became king of Wessex.

The Vikings scorned English kings like Burgred of Mercia, who offered gold for peace. They also disliked their enemies' religion. They murdered King Edmund of East Anglia when he refused to give up his Christian faith. The pagan Vikings looked set to triumph.

ALFRED OF WESSEX

Wessex was now the only kingdom still under Anglo-Saxon rule. The Vikings began their attack in 871, the year that King Ethelred I died. A Viking victory seemed certain. But the new king, Alfred, would not give in. His courage, determination, and skill saved Wessex and made it the foundation for a united kingdom of England.

Alfred knew his Viking enemies from fighting them in Mercia with Ethelred. But in the first battles for Wessex he was beaten and had to make peace. The victorious Vikings went north to fight rebels in Northumbria. Then in 875 a new Viking army arrived. Part of it again marched north. The rest, led by Guthrum, launched a new campaign against Wessex in 878.

The attack caught the men of Wessex by surprise. Most were at home on their farms. Almost all the kingdom surrendered, but not Alfred. He escaped to hide in the Somerset marshes and plan how to win back his kingdom. He gathered a new army, and in spring marched out to defeat the Vikings at Edington.

Alfred had four older brothers who were made king of Wessex in turn.
● Before he was 7 years old, Alfred twice went to visit the Pope in Rome.
● His mother promised a poetry book to the first son who could learn it by heart. Alfred won.
● Alfred learnt to read and write at 38 and then translated books from Latin to English. The Alfred Jewel (right) found in Somerset may be a marker sent with one of his books to a bishop. It says "Alfred had me made".
● Alfred's life history was written by a court scholar called Asser.

Alfred's greatness was clear, to his followers and his enemies. He had shown that the Vikings could be beaten. Now, hoping to keep the peace, he let Guthrum's men settle in East Anglia.

To make Wessex strong, Alfred built forts called burhs, which grew into thriving towns. He also gained support from his neighbours in Mercia and in Wales. When the Danes attacked Kent in 885, Alfred was able to overcome them. In 886 he led his victorious army into London and rebuilt the city walls. All the English now saw him as their king. He made good laws, restored monasteries, and had books written, in both Latin and English. For his achievements he is the only English king called "the great".

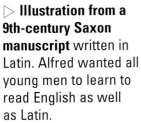

▷ **Illustration from a 9th-century Saxon manuscript** written in Latin. Alfred wanted all young men to learn to read English as well as Latin.

△ **After his defeat at Edington, Guthrum agreed to be baptized a Christian** (shown above left). He chose the name of Athelstan, and Alfred was his godfather.

The land held by the Vikings (Danes), as shown above, became known as the Danelaw. Here the laws in force were Danish, not Saxon.

THE KINGDOM OF WESSEX

Wessex was a wealthy kingdom with generous and just rulers who kept their people's loyalty. Unlike Mercia and Northumbria, it had not been split by quarrels between rival kings. This unity made it strong enough to defeat the Vikings and grow into the kingdom of England.

▷ **The burhs (forts) of Wessex** were laid out on a grid system like the one shown opposite. They included Winchester, Oxford, and Chichester.
● Local thanes oversaw their building and troops.
● In total, 25,000 men defended the burhs.
● Nowhere was more than a day's march (30 kilometres) from a burh.

▷ **Illustration from a Saxon calendar** of farmers at work. Farm produce was sold at markets in the burhs.

Alfred had to make Wessex's defences strong enough to fight off future Viking attacks. The Vikings used fortified camps as bases for their raids. Alfred now built a line of his own forts in Wessex. These were manned by soldiers and gave shelter to local people in time of attack. Some were based on old Roman forts or walled towns. Others were new towns built on open land.

The Vikings moved swiftly by sea, and over land on horses. To defeat them, Alfred had to build a fleet and improve his army and his fighting methods.

▽ **Farmers had to send two men** to the Wessex army for every plough they owned, or pay a fine. The king used money from fines to hire soldiers.

▽ **Saxon courts** often tried people by making them undergo nasty ordeals. One punishment was to be locked in stocks, as here.

The Anglo-Saxon Chronicle records that Alfred "divided his forces into two, so that there were always half of the men at home, half out on duty". It also says that Alfred ordered troop-carrying ships to be built. When the Vikings came back in 893, they were kept out of Wessex.

Local leaders saw that the king's orders were carried out. First among his officers were the ealdormen in charge of a shire. Kingdoms were made up of shires, and shires of "hundreds" (groups of 100 families). Thanes had local duties but also served for a month at Alfred's court. They then spent 2 months at home. Town officers called reeves collected taxes and kept law and order.

Alfred tried to weaken the custom of family feuds. By Saxon law, a man fleeing a feud could stay for 7 days in a church, but be given no food. A thief who stole from a church might have his hand cut off, or pay a fine according to his wergild. A thief caught in the king's hall paid a fine 24 times greater than a thief breaking into a cottage.

▽ **Alfred wanted priests to be well educated** once more. The Anglo-Saxon Chronicle was probably begun in his reign.

▽ **Alfred ordered new ships** to be built, each with a mast, sail, and 60 oars. Some of his sailors came from Frisia (now part of the Netherlands).

GUTHRUM AND THE DANELAW

In 878, the treaty of Wedmore was agreed between Alfred and Guthrum. It divided England between them. The Vikings settled in the eastern half, from Northumbria to Essex, where they set up homes and farms. The Viking leader of the Great Army was now a Christian. Would peace last?

△ **A Viking copy of an English penny.** Such coins were used for trade in the Danelaw.

Alfred probably did not trust the Vikings to honour the peace treaty. That is why he strengthened the defences of Wessex. But for a while at least, the Vikings (Danes) in the lands that became known as the Danelaw kept their word. They settled to peaceful village life. Some took English wives but they kept their own language and laws. Although it was no longer at war, Guthrum's Great Army kept troops in the fortified bases of Leicester, Nottingham, Derby, Stamford, and Lincoln. There was also a powerful Viking force in York (then called Jorvik).

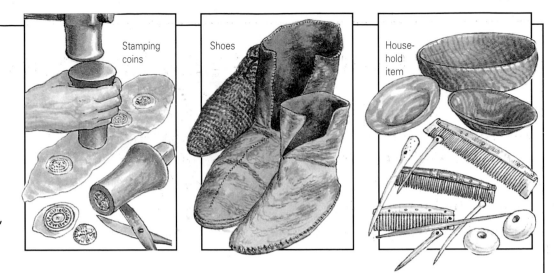
Stamping coins

Shoes

Household item

▷ **Vikings in England made some of the things** they needed and traded for other items.
● Coins were stamped at York and Lincoln.
● Shoes and belts were made from leather.
● Men wore shirts, tunics, and trousers of wool.
● Women wore a linen dress under a wool tunic.
● Household items included keys for locking chests, clothing pins, and kitchen knives.
● Food was stored in clay pots and served in wooden bowls.
● Combs were made from deer antler.

◁ **Village life in the Danelaw.** Settlers took over the lands and often the homes of English farmers who had fled.
● They ploughed and sowed the old strip fields, but did not work for a lord or nobleman.
● Some kept slaves to help with farmwork.
● They cut down trees for firewood and to sell timber to cart-makers and to house-builders in nearby towns such as York.
● They made hurdles of woven sticks, as shown opposite. The hurdles were used for fencing, screens around outdoor toilets, and to make paths across boggy ground.

The Vikings in England did not give up seafaring. Traders went on voyaging to the markets of the Continent and beyond, and there was a busy trade across the Irish Sea to Dublin. Town-life grew in the Danelaw. Towns such as Peterborough, Ely, Cambridge, and Norwich all became wealthy. They were centres of trade and later of Church life. In the countryside, the Viking farmer-warriors did much as they liked. They took local people as slaves, but were not willing to serve a lord. Viking nobles or jarls (earls) had less power than the English thanes.

The peace between English and Danes was brief. Three years after Guthrum's death in 890, Viking sea-raids began again. Danelaw farmers took up their swords to join these new raiders, eager to take land from their old foes, the West Saxons. But Alfred's army and his new navy fought off the attacks.

Fighting went on after Alfred's death in 899. But now the English had the upper hand. Alfred's son Edward led his army into Viking East Anglia in 902. He also defeated the Northumbrian Vikings. With help from his sister, Aethelflaed of Mercia, Edward won control of all the Danelaw.

A last threat came from Raegnald of Dublin, who made himself king of York in 919. But a year later the Viking king submitted to Edward. The Danelaw was now ruled by English kings, although York had Viking kings until 954.

JORVIK, A VIKING CITY

In 866 the Northumbrian city of York had fallen to the Viking army. Northumbria had been one of the great English kingdoms. Its capture seemed a disaster. But Viking York, or Jorvik, became the capital of a new kingdom, even richer and more powerful.

York had been a fort-city since Roman times. The Vikings laid out new streets in an area between the rivers Ouse and Foss. They built houses of wattle (woven sticks) with thatched roofs. They repaired parts of the Roman walls.

By AD 1000, as many as 10,000 people lived in Jorvik. Many were craftworkers selling their goods from shops. There were weavers and dyers of woollen cloth. Jewellers made rings and beads from amber, jet (a black stone), and glass, or brooches from gold and silver. Turners shaped wooden bowls and cups. Metalworkers melted gold, silver, and copper in furnaces. Coiners stamped coins. Leatherworkers cut out shoes and belts from ox-hides and deerskin.

▷ **Objects used by people in Jorvik** and found by archaeologists, as shown right, include:
● wooden tools and bowls
● leather shoes
● pieces of rope
● fragments of cloth
● ice skates made from bones
● coins from as far away as Asia
● metal tools such as leatherworkers' awls (used for making holes).

▽ **A street in Jorvik was smoky, smelly, and noisy.**
● Houses had a wood fire on a central hearth. They had wooden walls and wattle fences all around.
● Behind the houses were workshops, rubbish pits, wells, and pens for pigs, goats and chickens.

Foreign traders came to Jorvik from Dublin in Ireland, and from Norway, Sweden, and Iceland. Silks and coins from Asia have been found in the town. Archaeologists have even found a shell from the Arabian Gulf.

Many of the most interesting Viking remains in York were in an area called Coppergate, where cupmakers worked. The ground was wet, so wooden and leather objects did not rot but were preserved. In waste pits, archaeologists have found food remains such as pig, sheep, deer, chicken, pigeon, and fish bones, and shellfish shells, nutshells, eggshells, and cereal seeds.

The people of Jorvik enjoyed games. Children played a kind of football. Everyone liked horse racing, wrestling, and ice skating in winter. In summer they swam and had boat races on the river. The Vikings had three annual feasts: in early summer, at harvest time, and after mid-winter. Then people feasted, sang, and heard the stories of heroic deeds that all Vikings enjoyed.

▽ **People used outdoor toilets.** These had wattle walls. The seat was a board with a hole in it. Digging into the mud beneath the remains of these toilets, scientists have found clues to the kinds of foods people ate.

▽ **Women did the cooking**, in iron cauldrons or clay pots, over a fire in the hearth. They also baked bread and made butter and cheese. Vikings ate two main meals: breakfast and evening dinner.

Jorvik was a busy trading centre. Traders came in ships which sailed upriver from the North Sea, to berth at the waterfront and unload their cargoes. Merchants carried their own scales to weigh goods and coins.

THE SAXONS' GOLDEN AGE

Alfred and his sons made England one kingdom. The kings of Wessex could also demand the loyalty of kings in Wales and Scotland. In the reigns of Athelstan and Edgar, England was strong, peaceful, and well-governed.

Athelstan was Alfred's grandson. He became king in 924. In 937 he won a great battle at Brunanburh (somewhere near Carlisle) against an army of Irish Vikings, Scots, and Strathclyde Britons. The north was now firmly under control. Athelstan was the first Saxon king to command loyalty from all Britain.

Like Alfred, Athelstan was interested in good government. He ordered that one coinage should be used throughout the land. The burhs became centres of local government, with ealdormen ruling in the king's name. The king was a collector of art and holy relics, such as bones of saints. He was delighted to own the sword of the Roman emperor Constantine.

After Athelstan died in 939, his successors, Edmund and Eadred, had to fight new Viking raiders. England was not at peace again until Edgar became king of Wessex in 959. Edgar was all-powerful and won support from several Welsh and Scottish kings. He set up courts to keep law and order.

△▷ **The king with his council, or witan.**
● The witan agreed taxes for people to pay for the army and navy. It also advised on new laws made by the king.
● At local meetings, ordinary people could make complaints about laws.
● Laws were written in Latin, by monks.

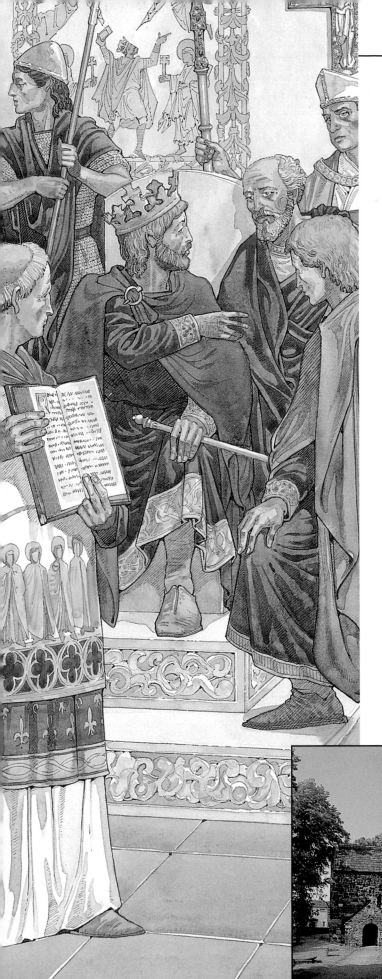

▷ **England's monasteries were reformed by Dunstan.** King Edgar sacked the old Archbishop of Canterbury and gave Dunstan the task. Edgar was protector of the Church and leader of its bishops. This is a Saxon chess bishop.

Edgar's chief advisor was Dunstan, Archbishop of Canterbury. Dunstan and Bishops Oswald of York and Ethelwold of Winchester made changes in the Church. Monasteries had been run by monks who had got into bad habits. Now monks had to live by strict rules. In 973, Edgar was crowned in a special religious ceremony at Bath.

Edgar died, aged only 32, in 975. The golden age ended. Now, a Saxon wrote sadly: "Strife threw the kingdom into turmoil... family against family."

◁ **Edgar's court at Winchester** was the centre of power in England and one of the most splendid in Europe.
● Princes from Wales and Scotland came there to show their loyalty.
● Nobles from all over England attended meetings of the witan, or king's council.
● The witan also included bishops.

◁ **The Saxon church at Escomb** near Durham. During the late 900s new churches like this, as well as many monasteries, were built in England. This upsurge of religious activity was partly because the country was at peace. Dunstan's revival of monastery life saw many books being produced.

VIKINGS TAKE THE CROWN

"There was no chief who would assemble forces, but each fled as he might," said the *Anglo-Saxon Chronicle* for 975. After Edgar's death, England fell into confusion and misery. Viking fleets returned, looting and destroying towns. In 1016, a Dane became king of England.

Edgar's son, Edward, became king in 975. A comet – a sign of troubled times, so people believed – was followed by a famine. Then in 978 Edward was murdered, probably by supporters of his young step-brother, Ethelred II, the Unready (from the English *unraed* meaning evil advice). Ethelred became king in 979, but the troubles continued.

Viking raids began in 980, and Ethelred tried to buy off the Danes. First, he raised taxes and handed over huge sums known as Danegeld, or Danes' gold. Then, he gave the Danish soldiers land on condition they fight for him. They demanded more. Ethelred ordered a massacre of Danes living in England and so angered the Danish king, Sweyn Forkbeard.

In 1013, Sweyn's army ravaged England and Ethelred fled to Normandy in France. The English nobles asked Sweyn to be their king. He accepted, but died in 1014 before being crowned.

The Viking invaders came:
● from Norway, led by Olaf Tryggvason, who later became king of Norway.
● from Denmark, led by the Danish king Sweyn Forkbeard.
Among the victims of the massacre of Danes in 1002 had been Sweyn's sister, Gunnhilda.

▽ **The major Viking raids** from about 980 to 1014.

Viking raids

from Norway
N
from Denmark
from Normandy

▷ **The Battle of Maldon in Essex in 991** between the English and invading Vikings led by Anlaf.
● The warriors faced each other across the River Blackwater. (Here, the English are on the mainland, the Vikings on an island reached by a causeway that was flooded at high tide.)
● The English leader, Byrhtnoth, let the Danes cross the causeway.
● The English fought to the last man after Byrhtnoth was killed.

Ethelred returned, but died in 1016. Sweyn's son, Cnut (or Canute), now led the Danish army in England. Ethelred's son, Edmund Ironside, fought the Danes so fiercely that Cnut agreed to share the kingdom with him. But Edmund died after only months as ruler, and Cnut became king of England.

England, with Denmark and Norway, was now part of a North Sea empire, and Cnut's power was recognized by the Welsh, Scots and Irish. Cnut brought peace but weakened royal power. When he visited his overseas kingdoms, he left the government of England to trusted earls. The most powerful and ambitious of these earls was Godwine of Wessex.

▷ **A silver penny of Ethelred the Unready.** Vast sums of English gold and silver were taken by the Vikings, as bribes and loot. Ethelred alone gave them over 8 tonnes weight of Danegeld, or Danes' gold.

△ **Cnut became king in 1016.** He began by having some of his enemies killed, but later governed well.
- He was a Christian and married Ethelred's widow, Emma.
- Many Danes settled in England. The Danish title "jarl" or "earl" replaced English "ealdorman".
- Cnut built warships, paid for by a land tax.
- Cnut's empire of Denmark, Norway, and England broke up after his death in 1035.

A STRUGGLE FOR POWER

Cnut's reign ended in 1035. For the next 30 years rivals schemed for the crown of England. Edward the Confessor built a great new church at Westminster. But his kingdom was weakened as ambitious men plotted against him at home and abroad.

Cnut's queen was Emma, who had also been married to Ethelred. Emma was from Normandy in France, and this made Cnut friendly with the powerful Duke of Normandy. When Cnut died, he left three sons: Harthacnut (Emma's son), Sweyn and Harold (sons by another wife). Emma had two more sons from her marriage to Ethelred, and they remained in Normandy. Which of these rivals would succeed Cnut? There was also rivalry between the great English earls – Leofric of Mercia, Siward of Northumbria and Godwine of Wessex. No one could become king without their support.

Queen Emma schemed for her sons in Normandy. One came to England, where he was attacked, blinded and died. His friends in Normandy blamed Earl Godwine for his death. In the end, Cnut's son Harold became king, but died in 1040. Harthacnut took over, but he died in 1042. There were no more Danish kings of England. Edward, son of Ethelred the Unready, came from Normandy to take the throne.

▷ **Edward was very religious,** and because he was always confessing his sins, he was called "The Confessor". Here he oversees the building of a great abbey church at Westminster near London. It was built in Norman style and finished in 1065.

◁ **Page from a herbal of about 1050.** It is in late Saxon style, before the influence of Norman culture.

Edward was more Norman than English, and brought with him Norman advisors. This caused jealousy. He married Earl Godwine's daughter, yet this did not bring peace with Wessex. Many people respected Edward as a just king, but he was not a strong ruler. Godwine died in 1053 and his son Harold became earl of Wessex. He, too, disliked Edward.

Edward had no children. Once again, no-one knew who would be the next king. The man with the power was Earl Harold of Wessex. But in Normandy and Norway there were other men with claims to the throne of England, and with armies to back them.

▽ **On Edward's death**, William of Normandy and Harold, earl of Wessex, became rivals for the throne of England.

William:
● was the son of Duke Robert of Normandy.
● had visited Edward the Confessor and later claimed the king had made him his heir.
● had the support of the Church in Rome.

Harold:
● was the most powerful earl in England.
● in about 1064 had visited William. The Normans said he swore an oath to support William's claim to England.
● in 1066 had been named by Edward as his successor (as in a scene from the Bayeux Tapestry, left).
● had the support of the English witan or council.

THE NORMANS INVADE

Edward the Confessor died in January 1066, and the English witan chose Harold of Wessex as king. But William of Normandy and Harald Hardrada of Norway also claimed a right to the crown. Both prepared to invade England and seize it.

William of Normandy was a distant relative of Edward the Confessor. But the two men were very different. William was no saint, while his father, Duke Robert, was nicknamed "the Devil". William had learned to be a ruthless soldier. He had fought rivals to master Normandy, and he was ready to fight for the English crown he claimed Edward had promised him.

The witan seems to have known nothing about Edward's promise to William. The Archbishop of Canterbury agreed that Edward had named Harold of Wessex as the next king, and Harold prepared to fight for the crown. But he had already lost the support of his brother, Tostig, earl of Northumbria. Tostig had so upset the Northumbrians that there was a risk of civil war and Harold was forced to send him away. Tostig then turned against his brother and fled to join Harald Hardrada's army, which had landed in the north of England as the Normans waited to cross the Channel.

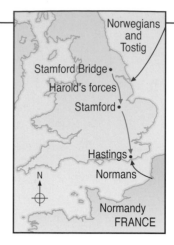

△ **The invasions of 1066.**
● Harald Hardrada landed in north-east England, joined by Tostig.
● On 25 September, the English defeated the Norwegians.
● On 28 September the Normans landed in Sussex.
● On 14 October, Harold lost the battle of Hastings.

▽ **The Battle of Hastings and the events leading up to it** are recorded on the Bayeux Tapestry. This part of the tapestry shows Norman horsemen charging.

△ **At Stamford Bridge**, Harold's forces defeated the Norwegians. Then Harold hurried south to fight William (right).

△▷ **At Hastings, William's forces**, brought from Normandy by boat, as shown right, beat the English soldiers.

Harold led his men north to fight the Norwegians and Tostig. At the battle of Stamford Bridge near York the English won a great victory. Harald Hardrada and Tostig were among the dead. Now came the grim news that the Normans had landed in Sussex. Harold rushed south, with his weary army, to drive William into the sea. Some thanes held back, but others sent fresh troops to aid their new king. Harold did not wait for them. On 14 October the English met the Norman invaders on Senlac Hill near Hastings. Harold was killed. William had conquered, and in one battle ended the Saxon rule of England. He was crowned king on Christmas Day 1066.

At Hastings:
● The English stood shield to shield on a hilltop.
● Norman archers fired arrows as their foot-soldiers charged uphill.
● The Normans faked retreats to lure the English into their cavalry.
● Harold was killed, perhaps by an arrow in the eye (below).

FAMOUS SAXONS AND VIKINGS

Aidan (died 651) was an Irish monk and first Bishop of Lindisfarne (see page 17).

Alcuin (**Albinus**) (735?–804) was an English scholar who helped Charlemagne of the Franks revive learning in western Europe.

Alfred the Great (849–899) was king of the West Saxons and recognized as ruler of all England. He fought the Danes, encouraged learning, and made wise laws (see pages 28–29).

Athelstan (895–939), Alfred's grandson and king of England, was one of the great kings of his time. He beat the Scots, Welsh, and Irish Vikings at the battle of Brunanburh in 937 (see page 36).

Augustine, Saint (died 604) was sent by Pope Gregory I to convert the English to Christianity. He was the first Archbishop of Canterbury (see page 16).

Saint Augustine

Bede (673–735) was an English monk and scholar. He lived in the monastery at Jarrow in north-east England and wrote *The Ecclesiastical History of the English People,* a history of England.

Brian Boru (died 1014) was Christian king of Ireland; he was slain by fleeing Vikings after his army had won the battle of Clontarf.

Cadwallon (died 634) was king of Gwynedd, west Wales and fought with Penda of Mercia to defeat the Northumbrian king, Edwin (see page 18). Edwin's nephew killed Cadwallon.

Charlemagne (742–814) was Christian king of the Franks from 768 and emperor of the West Roman Empire from 800. He was a great soldier and patron of learning. His empire traded with the kingdoms of England during Offa's reign (see page 19).

Cnut or Canute (about 995–1035) was a Danish-born king of England (from 1016) and also of Denmark. and Norway. He won the throne by war, but brought peace (see page 39).

Columba, Saint (522–597) was an Irish Christian missionary to northern Britain. He founded a monastery on the island of Iona (see page 17).

Cuthbert, Saint (about 635–687) was an English monk and Bishop of Lindisfarne (see page 17). After his death, his body was believed to work miracles.

Dunstan, Saint (about 920–988) was a Wessex-born churchman who practically ruled England as Archbishop of Canterbury during the reigns of Eadwig and Edgar (see page 37).

Edward the Confessor (1003–1066) was king of England from 1042 (see page 40). A religious man, he was the son of King Ethelred the Unready.

Godwine (died 1053) was Earl of Wessex and father of Harold II. He was the most powerful nobleman in England (see pages 39, 40).

Gruffydd ap Llywelyn (1039–1063) was first king of all Wales, and fought off English efforts to seize Welsh lands.

Guthrum (died 890) was leader of the Danes who made peace with Alfred and settled in East Anglia (see pages 28, 29).

Harold II, Earl of Wessex (about 1022–1066), was elected king of England in 1066 but killed at the battle of Hastings (see page 43).

Hywel Dda (Howel the Good, died 950) was king of Wales and a great law-maker. He succeeded in uniting the kingdoms of Gwynedd, Powys, and Dyfed. A friend of the English kings, he was Rhodri Mawr's grandson.

Kenneth McAlpin (died 860) was the king of the West Scots (843–60). He drove the Vikings from his lands and made Scone (near Perth on the River Tay) his new capital.

Malcolm II (died 1034) was king of Scots 1005–34. He captured Strathclyde and Lothian, and in so doing helped shape modern Scotland.

Offa (died 796) was king of Mercia from 757, a soldier and law-maker admired by Charlemagne (see page 18).

Offa

Patrick, Saint (about 389–461) spread the Christian faith in Ireland, of which he is patron saint (see page 17).

Redwald (died about 627) was king of East Anglia and probably the ruler for whom the Sutton Hoo ship burial was made (see pages 14–15).

Rhodri Mawr (Rodric the Great, died 878) was king of Gwynedd from 844 and fought the Vikings in west Wales.

William the Conqueror (1027–1087), son of Duke Robert of Normandy in France, was ruler of Normandy from 1035 and after his successful invasion, king of England from 1066 (see page 42).

William the Conqueror

KINGS, KINGDOMS, AND PLACE NAMES

Kings of Scotland (from 843)
Kenneth McAlpin or
    Macalpine (843–860)
Donald I (860–864)
Constantine I (864–877)
Aedh (877–878)
Euche (878–889)
Donald II (889–900)
Constantine II (900–942)
Malcolm I (942–954)
Indulphus (954–962)
Duff (962–967)
Culen (967–971)
Kenneth II (971–995)
Constantine III (995–997)
Kenneth III (997–1005)
Malcolm II (1005–1034)
Duncan I (1034–1040)
Macbeth (1040–1057)
Malcolm III (1057–1093)

Princes of Wales (from 844)
Rhodri Mawr (844–878)
Anarawd (878–916)
Hywel Dda (916–950)
Iago ap Idwal (950–979)
Hywel ap Leuaf (979–985)
Cadwallon (985–986)
Maredudd ap Owain ap Hywel
    Dda (986–999)
Cynan ap Hywel ap Ieuaf
    (999–1008)
Llywelyn ap Seisyll (1018–1023)
Lago ap Idwal ap Meurig
    (1023–1039)
Gruffydd ap Llywelyn
    (1039–1063)
Bleddyn (1063–1075)

Wessex royal family
Egbert or Ecbert (828–839)
Ethelwulf or Aethelwulf (839–856)
Ethelbald or Aethelbald (856–860)
Ethelbert or Aethelbert (860–866)
Ethelred or Aethelred I (866–871)
Alfred the Great (871–900)
Edward the Elder (900–924)
Athelstan (924–940)
Edmund I (940–946)
Eadred (946–955)
Eadwig (955–959)
Edgar or Eadgar (959–975)
Edward the Martyr (975–978)
Ethelred or Aethelred II, the
    Unready (978–1016)
Edmund II, Ironside (1016)
Danish
Cnut or Canute (1016–1035)
Harold I, Harefoot (1035–1040)
Harthacnut or Harthacanute
    (1040–1042)
Wessex
Edward the Confessor (1042–1066)
Harold II (1066)
Norman
William I, the Conqueror
    (1066–1087)

Place names
Below is a list of some common endings in present-day names for villages and towns which come from words used by the Angles, Saxons, and Vikings:
- bury, burgh, borough (a fortified area)
- dale (valley)
- fell (large hill)
- ford (a shallow part of a river)
- ham (a homestead)
- hurst (a wood)
- ing (people of)
- ley, leigh or leagh (a clearing in a forest)
- thwaite (a meadow)
- ton or toft (a farm and its buildings)
- wick or wich (group of houses)

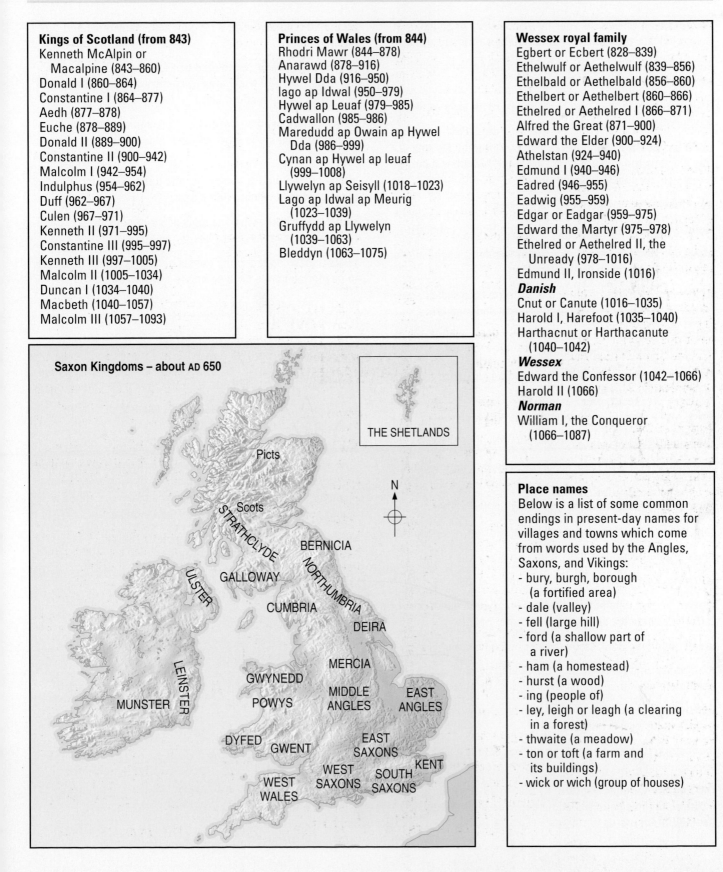

Saxon Kingdoms – about AD 650

THE SHETLANDS

N

Picts
Scots
STRATHCLYDE
ULSTER
GALLOWAY
BERNICIA
NORTHUMBRIA
CUMBRIA
DEIRA
LEINSTER
MERCIA
GWYNEDD
MIDDLE ANGLES
EAST ANGLES
MUNSTER
POWYS
DYFED
GWENT
EAST SAXONS
KENT
WEST SAXONS
SOUTH SAXONS
WEST WALES

GLOSSARY

Anglo-Saxon Chronicle year-by-year history of England, begun in 800s and continued until 1100s, written by monks

Beowulf long Old English poem about a hero who fights monsters, written about 750

bishop leader in the Church, in charge of an area called a diocese

burh fortified town, first developed by Alfred of Wessex. It has given us the modern term "borough", which is a part of a city with its own local government.

cauldron large iron pot used for cooking

Celts people living in Britain before the Roman conquest

charcoal partly burnt wood, used in furnaces, especially for iron-making, because it gets very hot

craftsmen people who earned their living by a skill or special trade, such as blacksmiths, potters, and shoemakers

Danegeld money paid by English kings to Danish Vikings, to stop them attacking their lands

Danelaw land in eastern England settled by Danish Vikings, given them by King Alfred

dyke steep bank of earth built as a defence

feud quarrel carried on by members of rival families

freeman ordinary person; someone who is neither a slave nor a thane

frontier boundary between one kingdom and another

jarl Viking lord or chieftain; jarl became "earl"

loom frame used to weave cloth

longship Viking warship, with oars and one sail

martyr person who suffers great pain, or even death, from torture to show the strength of his or her beliefs

mead alcoholic drink made from honey and water

merchants people who made their living by buying and selling things, either in their own country or abroad

missionary person travelling to and teaching in distant lands to spread his or her religion

monastery buildings lived in by monks, who are men devoted to religious life

Old English language spoken by the Anglo-Saxons; in different regions people pronounced words differently or used different words for things

pagan person following a religion with many gods and nature spirits

reeve local official, appointed by a chief or monarch. The reeve of a shire (a small area of countryside), a "shire-reeve", has given us the modern word "sheriff".

runes letters used by Saxons and Vikings to write on memorial stones and other objects, made by cutting straight lines

slave person who is owned by, and has to work for, another person, usually without being paid

smith metalworker making tools and weapons of iron, often believed to have magical skills

taxes money collected by nobles and kings from the people to pay for buildings or to equip the army and navy

thane Saxon nobleman who owned land and was sworn to fight for his king

treaty agreement between two sides, for example, to end a war

tunic long jacket with short sleeves and no buttons

wattle building material made from woven sticks, often covered with mud or plaster (daub)

wergild in Saxon times, the value of a person's life. This amount of money had to be paid by a convicted killer of the person to the victim's family. Convicted thieves were fined amounts according to their wergilds; a thane was fined a higher sum than a freeman for the same crime.

witan king's council in Saxon England

FIND OUT MORE

BOOKS

Anglo-Saxon Raiders and Settlers, Brian Knapp (Atlantic Europe, 2005)

Eyewitness: Viking, Susan Margeson (Dorling Kindersley, 2005)

Family Life: Saxon Britain, Peter Hicks (Hodder, 1994)

Life in Britain: Anglo-Saxon and Viking Britain, Fiona Macdonald (Franklin Watts, 2003)

What Happened Here?: Anglo-Saxon Village, Monica Stoppleman (A & C Black, 2000)

WEBSITES

www.bbc.co.uk/schools/anglosaxons/index.shtml
Find out how the Anglo-Saxons lived.

www.britainexpress.com
Scroll down to the "History and Culture" section for a list of Anglo-Saxon websites.

www.britannia.com/history/index.html
A list of websites and pages, including maps of the period and much more.

www.channel4.com/learning
Search under "Saxons" or "Vikings" for features on all aspects of life at the time.

www.great-britain.co.uk
Click on "Anglo-Saxon" for a huge range of articles.

PLACES TO VISIT

In museums all over Britain, especially in places settled by Saxons and Vikings, you can see objects from these times, such as coins, jewellery, weapons, pottery, and coins. There are also some ancient buildings and monuments, such as stone crosses. These are some of the best places to visit:

British Library, London   Illuminated manuscripts including the Lindisfarne Gospel are on display here.

British Museum, London   Sutton Hoo treasures and other finds can be seen here.

Dublin, Ireland   The Book of Kells in the University College Library is a beautiful early manuscript.

Durham, Northumbria   This Norman cathedral contains the embroidered vestment of St Cuthbert.

Iona, Hebrides, Scotland   St Columba's cell, Viking burial ground, and stone crosses can all be found on this island.

Museum of London, London   Viking weapons and other finds are on display here.

Offa's Dyke, border of England and Wales   Parts of the Dyke are still clearly visible.

Waterford, Ireland   A Viking town with Norman buildings.

West Stow, Suffolk   Modern reconstruction of a Saxon village.

York, North Yorkshire   The Jorvik Viking Centre contains reconstructions of life in Viking town.

INDEX